21st Century Junior Library

SPEAKING OUT CREATING CHANGE

Read and Reflect: A Social-Emotional Guide

Emily Rose

Published in the United States of America by:

CHERRY LAKE PRESS
2395 South Huron Parkway, Suite 200, Ann Arbor, Michigan 48104
www.cherrylakepress.com

Reading Adviser: Beth Walker Gambro, MS, Ed., Reading Consultant, Yorkville, IL
Photo Credits: © ViDI Studio/Shutterstock.com, cover, 1; © wavebreakmedia/Shutterstock.com, 5; © Diego Cervo/Shutterstock.com, 6; © Solis Images/Shutterstock.com, 7; © SpeedKingz/Shutterstock.com, 8; © Africa Studio/Shutterstock.com, 9; © pathdoc/Shutterstock.com, 10, 11; © VCoscaron/Shutterstock.com, 13 [top]; © Droidworker/Shutterstock.com, 13 [bottom, right]; © jesadaphorn/Shutterstock.com, 13 [bottom, left]; © Bricolage/Shutterstock.com, 14; © Prostock-studio/Shutterstock.com, 16; © Aniwhite/Shutterstock.com, 18; © TashaNatasha/Shutterstock.com, 19; © Zety Hasbi Sahin/Shutterstock.com, 20 [right]; © Akhzar/Shutterstock.com, 20 [left]; © Cheksii Synelnykov/Shutterstock.com, 21

Cherry Lake Press is an imprint of Cherry Lake Publishing Group.

Library of Congress Cataloging-in-Publication Data

Names: Rose, Emily (School psychologist), author.
Title: Speaking out and creating change / by Emily Rose.
Description: Ann Arbor, Michigan : Cherry Lake Publishing, [2022] | Series: Read and reflect: a social-emotional guide | Includes bibliographical references and index. | Audience: Grades 2-3
Identifiers: LCCN 2021036770 (print) | LCCN 2021036771 (ebook) | ISBN 9781534199132 (hardcover) | ISBN 9781668900277 (paperback) | ISBN 9781668906033 (ebook) | ISBN 9781668901717 (pdf)
Subjects: LCSH: Social change—Juvenile literature. | Change (Psychology)—Juvenile literature.
Classification: LCC HM831 .R667 2022 (print) | LCC HM831 (ebook) | DDC 303.4—dc23
LC record available at https://lccn.loc.gov/2021036770
LC ebook record available at https://lccn.loc.gov/2021036771

Cherry Lake Press would like to acknowledge the work of the Partnership for 21st Century Learning, a Network of Battelle for Kids. Please visit http://www.battelleforkids.org/networks/p21 for more information.

Printed in the United States of America
Corporate Graphics

CHERRY LAKE PRESS

CONTENTS

BEING AN UPSTANDER INSTEAD OF A BYSTANDER

We are taught in school to stand up to bullies and do the right thing when we see something that can hurt someone else. It's not always easy, but the first step to making positive change is to speak up. People are called bystanders when they are around when something unjust happens. There is a new

Describe a time when you were a bystander and saw something unjust or unfair happening.

term for bystanders who **intervene**, or speak up when something bad is happening. They are called upstanders!

Think of a time when you saw someone be an upstander. What did that person do to help someone in need?

How do you like to learn new things? Brainstorm ways like watching educational videos, reading books, and listening to your teacher.

An upstander is someone who sees something unfair, unjust, or hurtful happening and says or does something to stop it from continuing. If you hear someone call your friend a mean name,

you can be an upstander by saying something like, "Hey, stop that! What you are saying is hurtful." If you see a kid being left out of a game on the playground, you can ask them to join you and your friends.

Make a Guess!

Now that you know what it means to be an upstander, think about how you could respond if you saw something unjust happening. What things could you say or do to intervene?

Can you think of a time you stood up for a friend?

LEARN ABOUT THINGS THAT MIGHT BE UNEQUAL

It is easy to know when someone says something mean or hurtful that we should intervene, but sometimes we might not notice *every* situation that could use an upstander or a **change agent** to help. We all come from different cultures, different experiences, and different **privileges**, depending on where we live. And because we are all different, we might know more about some things and not as much about other things. Nobody can know

everything, but everyone can learn and become a better **citizen** to understand how to help everyone.

For example, when the United States became a country, only men with white skin could vote in elections. Now, everyone born in America is born with the right to vote. This is because people spoke out against this unfair **policy**. They fought for voting **equality**, which helped make the country more fair for everyone. We understand what types of inequality or unfairness exist only when we learn about history. Otherwise, how would we know which things need us to act as an upstander to change?

What unfair things can you think of that could use some positive change?

Once we are aware of the problems that exist, then we can start to use our voices to **advocate** for what is right. Just like people once did to **achieve** voting equality! You can learn about history by reading books, watching educational videos or movies, and asking your history teacher questions.

Look!

What unfair policies do you know about that have been changed to be more equal for everyone? (Hint: voting equality is one!) These policies can be something in your school or something in the world.

When you think of making positive change in the world, how does it make you feel?

HOW TO START MAKING POSITIVE CHANGE

Once we learn about the unfair things in the world that need our help in order to change, it can feel overwhelming, or way too big for us to solve. When we feel like this, it's helpful to remember that no one can solve all the problems in the world alone, but each one of us can do something small. All the small things added together can make a big difference. It's important to understand that it's not your responsibility to do *everything*, but it is everyone's responsibility to do *something*!

Practice speaking up when you see something unfair or hurtful happening. Say you learn about a problem in the world, such as plastic waste in the oceans. You can ask your teacher if your class or school can start a **campaign** to raise money for an **organization** that cleans the oceans. Or start a class challenge to see which class can pick up the most litter during Earth month or even every month!

What things do you care about in the world? Things like keeping Earth clean or stopping bullies at school are some examples to get your brain thinking.

You can also make positive changes in your home. Maybe you learn about food waste that goes in the garbage but could go in gardens to help make soil healthier for growing plants. You can talk to your parents about researching how to start a **compost** bin in your backyard or donating your food scraps to a local community garden! This is another great example of doing good exactly where you are to make positive change.

Start small by speaking up exactly where you are in the world with exactly the things that you care about. You will probably inspire others to speak up more too. Soon enough, positive changes will start to happen!

Think!

How can you speak up or get involved to make some positive change? Think of the smallest first step you could take to make a positive change in an area that you really care about.

EXTEND YOUR LEARNING

Let's use our imaginations for a minute.

Pretend you see another kid on your soccer team throw her juice box on the ground after the snack break. You know that littering is bad for the planet, and you want to try to be an upstander and say something to your friend. Brainstorm what things you could say or do to make a positive change or action in this situation.

Now pretend that a student named Rob pushed down another student at recess. You know that Rob

can be a bully, and you're afraid to say something to him yourself. What else could you do to be an upstander in this situation?

Finally, let's think of a bigger world problem that we can help with—hunger. Not every family has enough money to buy all the food that they need, and some people go hungry. This is a big problem that takes a lot of steps to solve. What is one small step you can think of to help solve this problem in your community?

GLOSSARY

achieve **(uh-CHEEV)** to get or accomplish something

advocate **(AD-vuh-kuht)** to act in support of something

campaign **(kam-PAYN)** action to raise awareness about something or someone

change agent **(CHAYNJ AY-juhnt)** someone who creates positive change

citizen **(SIH-tuh-zuhn)** a legal member of a state or country

compost **(KAHM-pohst)** a mixture of organic substances such as leaves or food scraps that fertilize the soil

equality **(ih-KWAH-luh-tee)** the state of being equal; having the same rights as others

intervene **(in-tuhr-VEEN)** to come between or interrupt something

organization **(or-guh-nuh-ZAY-shuhn)** a structured group or company

policy **(PAH-luh-see)** a rule, procedure, or way of doing something

privileges **(PRIV-lij-uhs)** unearned and sometimes unnoticed advantages

FIND OUT MORE

Books

Mantchev, Lisa. *Strictly No Elephants.* New York, NY: Simon & Schuster, 2015.

Nagara, Innosanto. *A is for Activist.* New York, NY: Seven Stories Press, 2013.

Reynolds, Peter H. *Say Something!.* New York, NY: Orchard Books, 2019.

Websites

Be an Upstander

https://bullybust.org/students/upstander
Learn how to stand up to bullies with this resource.

YouTube—How to Change the World (A Work in Progress): Kid President

https://www.youtube.com/watch?v=4z7gDsSKUmU
Learn how to change the world.

YouTube—Malala and Teen Activists on Learning to Speak Out

https://www.youtube.com/watch?v=5fLaAEMeb90
Malala Yousafzai and other young activists discuss how they got started speaking out against injustice.

INDEX

ABOUT THE AUTHOR

Emily Rose is a school psychologist, yoga teacher, and writer for her mental wellness blog, MissMagnoliaSays.com. She enjoys helping kids and adults understand and manage their emotions and live beautiful lives. Emily lives in Dearborn, Michigan.